EMMANUEL JOSEPH

The Sovereign Algorithm, Billionaires, Blockchain, and the New Rules of Global Leadership

Copyright © 2025 by Emmanuel Joseph

All rights reserved. No part of this publication may be reproduced, stored or transmitted in any form or by any means, electronic, mechanical, photocopying, recording, scanning, or otherwise without written permission from the publisher. It is illegal to copy this book, post it to a website, or distribute it by any other means without permission.

First edition

This book was professionally typeset on Reedsy. Find out more at reedsy.com

Contents

1	Chapter 1: The Rise of the Sovereign Algorithm	1
2	Chapter 2: The Dawn of Blockchain: A New Era	3
3	Chapter 3: From Code to Currency: The Birth of...	5
4	Chapter 4: Billionaires and Blockchain: The New Titans	7
5	Chapter 5: The Decentralized Revolution: Power to the People	9
6	Chapter 6: Smart Contracts: The Future of Agreements	11
7	Chapter 7: DAOs: The New Organizational Model	13
8	Chapter 8: Blockchain and Global Governance	15
9	Chapter 9: The Impact on Traditional Industries	17
10	Chapter 10: The Financial Sector Transformed	19
11	Chapter 11: From Wall Street to Silicon Valley	21
12	Chapter 12: Blockchain in Emerging Markets	23
13	Chapter 13: Ethics and the Blockchain	25
14	Chapter 14: Security and Privacy Concerns	27
15	Chapter 15: The Road Ahead: Challenges and Opportunities	29
16	Chapter 16: Case Studies: Successes and Failures	31
17	Chapter 17: Conclusion: Embracing the New Rules of Global...	33

1

Chapter 1: The Rise of the Sovereign Algorithm

In the dimly lit corridors of global financial power, a seismic shift was brewing. The rise of blockchain technology and the decentralized digital currency it spawned, threatened to upend centuries of financial orthodoxy. Amid this technological revolution stood a silent sovereign—an algorithm, meticulously coded, dispensing trust through cryptographic proofs rather than human intermediaries. This sovereign algorithm was the genesis of a new world order, redefining the concepts of power and wealth.

The sovereign algorithm's influence rapidly transcended digital spaces, infiltrating the physical world with unprecedented force. Financial magnates and tech billionaires recognized its potential to disrupt the status quo. Traditional financial systems, long plagued by inefficiencies and centralization, began to crumble under the pressure of this unyielding digital force. The algorithm's promise of a decentralized, borderless economy was too compelling to ignore, and those who resisted its call risked obsolescence.

In this brave new world, blockchain technology became the backbone of the global economy, ensuring transparency, security, and efficiency in financial transactions. Cryptocurrencies, once a niche curiosity, evolved into mainstream assets, attracting the attention of institutional investors and governments alike. The allure of a decentralized financial system, free from the constraints of traditional banking, was a powerful motivator for adoption.

Yet, the rise of the sovereign algorithm was not without its challenges. Regulatory bodies scrambled to understand and control this new technology, grappling with its implications for monetary policy, taxation, and global trade. The tension between innovation and regulation created a complex landscape, where the stakes were high, and the future uncertain. In this volatile environment, the true power brokers emerged—those who could harness the algorithm's potential while navigating the treacherous waters of compliance and governance.

2

Chapter 2: The Dawn of Blockchain: A New Era

In the digital dawn of the 21st century, a revolutionary concept emerged from the mind of a mysterious figure known only as Satoshi Nakamoto. Blockchain technology, the backbone of Bitcoin, promised to redefine the foundations of trust, ownership, and value. Satoshi's whitepaper, published in 2008, outlined a peer-to-peer electronic cash system that bypassed traditional financial intermediaries. This bold vision was a response to the global financial crisis, which had exposed the fragility of centralized institutions.

Blockchain's genius lay in its decentralized and immutable ledger system. By distributing transaction data across a network of nodes, it ensured transparency, security, and resistance to tampering. Each block, once verified and added to the chain, was cryptographically linked to its predecessor, creating an unbroken and unalterable record of events. This innovation transcended the realm of digital currency, offering potential applications in fields as diverse as supply chain management, healthcare, and voting systems.

As the first blockchain-based cryptocurrency, Bitcoin captured the imagination of tech enthusiasts, libertarians, and visionaries alike. Early adopters recognized its potential to democratize finance and disrupt existing power structures. Bitcoin's meteoric rise in value and popularity spurred the development of alternative cryptocurrencies, collectively known as altcoins. Ethereum, launched in 2015, introduced smart contracts—self-executing agreements with the terms directly written into code—further expanding the possibilities of blockchain technology.

The dawn of blockchain marked a paradigm shift in how society conceptualized and interacted with digital assets. It challenged the traditional notions of trust, ownership, and authority, paving the way for a decentralized future. However, this new era also brought forth significant challenges and questions. How would existing legal and regulatory frameworks adapt to this disruptive force? What were the ethical implications of a technology that could potentially bypass government oversight and enable illicit activities?

Despite these uncertainties, the promise of blockchain technology was undeniable. As developers, entrepreneurs, and policymakers grappled with its complexities, one thing became clear: the genie was out of the bottle, and there was no turning back. The dawn of blockchain had ushered in a new era, one that would fundamentally reshape the fabric of global society.

3

Chapter 3: From Code to Currency: The Birth of Cryptocurrency

The concept of cryptocurrency began as an ambitious experiment a digital currency, untethered from any central authority, governed purely by mathematical algorithms and cryptographic protocols. The cryptographic community had long toyed with the idea of digital money, but it was Satoshi Nakamoto's Bitcoin that brought the vision to life. In January 2009, the first block, known as the Genesis Block, was mined, marking the birth of cryptocurrency.

Bitcoin's underlying technology, blockchain, provided a decentralized ledger that recorded transactions in a transparent and immutable manner. The brilliance of Bitcoin lay in its consensus mechanism, known as Proof of Work (PoW). This process required network participants, called miners, to solve complex mathematical puzzles to validate transactions and secure the network. In return, miners were rewarded with newly minted bitcoins. This ingenious system ensured the integrity of the blockchain without the need for a central authority.

In the early days, Bitcoin was met with skepticism and ridicule. Critics dismissed it as a fad or a tool for illicit activities. However, a small but dedicated community of believers saw its potential to revolutionize finance. Bitcoin's decentralization promised to eliminate intermediaries, reduce transaction costs, and provide financial inclusion to the unbanked. It was a radical departure from traditional monetary systems, which were often plagued by inefficiencies and vulnerabilities.

As Bitcoin gained traction, its value surged, attracting the attention of investors and the media. Stories of early adopters becoming millionaires overnight fueled a frenzy of interest. However, the volatility of the cryptocurrency market also led to wild price swings, prompting concerns about its stability and sustainability. Despite these challenges, Bitcoin's underlying principles inspired a wave of innovation and the creation of alternative cryptocurrencies.

Ethereum, launched by Vitalik Buterin in 2015, built upon Bitcoin's foundation but introduced a new paradigm: programmable money. Through smart contracts, Ethereum enabled developers to create decentralized applications (dApps) that could run on its blockchain. This innovation unlocked a multitude of use cases, from decentralized finance (DeFi) to non-fungible tokens (NFTs), further expanding the possibilities of blockchain technology.

The birth of cryptocurrency marked the beginning of a new financial era, where code could create and manage value without the need for traditional institutions. It was a bold experiment that challenged the very essence of money, governance, and trust. As cryptocurrencies continued to evolve and proliferate, they would shape the future of finance in ways that were still being discovered.

4

Chapter 4: Billionaires and Blockchain: The New Titans

In the rapidly evolving world of blockchain and cryptocurrency, a new class of titans emerged: the blockchain billionaires. These individuals, often technologists and visionaries, amassed significant wealth by embracing the disruptive potential of blockchain technology. Unlike traditional billionaires, whose fortunes were built on industries like finance, manufacturing, or real estate, these new titans built their empires on the foundations of code and cryptographic innovation.

Prominent figures like Vitalik Buterin, the creator of Ethereum, and Changpeng Zhao, the founder of Binance, became household names in the blockchain community. Their success stories were emblematic of the transformative power of blockchain, and their influence extended far beyond the digital realm. These billionaires wielded their newfound wealth and power to shape the future of technology, finance, and governance, often championing decentralized principles and challenging the status quo.

The rise of blockchain billionaires also highlighted the potential for significant social impact. Many of these individuals were driven by a desire to create positive change in the world. Initiatives like the Giving Pledge, founded by Bill Gates and Warren Buffett, found new adherents among the blockchain elite. These billionaires used their resources to fund projects aimed at addressing global challenges such as poverty, education, and healthcare, leveraging blockchain technology to create innovative solutions.

However, the ascent of blockchain billionaires was not without controversy. Critics argued that the concentration of wealth in the hands of a few contradicted the decentralized ethos of blockchain technology. The volatility of the cryptocurrency market also raised concerns about the sustainability of their fortunes and the potential for market manipulation. As the debate around wealth inequality and the role of technology in society continued, the actions of these new titans would be closely scrutinized.

Ultimately, the influence of blockchain billionaires extended beyond their financial success. They were pioneers in a new era, leveraging technology to create unprecedented opportunities and challenges. Their journeys served as a testament to the transformative power of blockchain and the potential for individuals to shape the course of history through innovation and vision.

5

Chapter 5: The Decentralized Revolution: Power to the People

The decentralized revolution, driven by blockchain technology, promised to shift power away from centralized institutions and into the hands of individuals. At its core, decentralization was about democratizing access to information, resources, and opportunities. By eliminating intermediaries and enabling peer-to-peer interactions, blockchain technology sought to create a more equitable and transparent world.

One of the most significant impacts of decentralization was in the realm of finance. Decentralized finance (DeFi) platforms allowed individuals to lend, borrow, and trade assets without relying on traditional banks. These platforms, built on blockchain technology, offered lower fees, greater accessibility, and increased transparency compared to conventional financial institutions. DeFi's rapid growth showcased the potential for blockchain to disrupt the global financial system and empower individuals to take control of their financial futures.

Beyond finance, decentralization had far-reaching implications for governance and decision-making. Decentralized Autonomous Organizations (DAOs) emerged as a new model for collective decision-making, where stakeholders could vote on proposals and influence the direction of the organization. DAOs leveraged smart contracts to ensure transparency and accountability, enabling more democratic and efficient governance structures. This shift towards decentralized governance had the potential to reshape industries, communities, and even nations.

The decentralized revolution also extended to data ownership and privacy. Traditional centralized systems often required users to relinquish control of their data to third parties, raising concerns about privacy and security. Blockchain technology offered a solution by enabling individuals to own and control their data, using cryptographic techniques to ensure its security. This empowerment of individuals to manage their digital identities was a fundamental aspect of the decentralized revolution.

While the promise of decentralization was compelling, it also faced significant challenges. The transition from centralized to decentralized systems required overcoming technical, regulatory, and cultural barriers. Ensuring the scalability and security of decentralized platforms was a complex and ongoing process. Additionally, the decentralized ethos of blockchain technology sometimes clashed with existing power structures, leading to resistance and pushback.

Despite these challenges, the decentralized revolution represented a profound shift in how society organized and interacted. By placing power in the hands of individuals, blockchain technology had the potential to create a more equitable and transparent world. As the decentralized revolution continued to unfold, it would redefine the boundaries of possibility and reshape the fabric of global society.

6

Chapter 6: Smart Contracts: The Future of Agreements

Smart contracts represented a groundbreaking evolution in the world of blockchain technology. These self-executing agreements, with the terms directly written into code, eliminated the need for intermediaries and ensured that contracts were automatically enforced when predefined conditions were met. The advent of smart contracts promised to revolutionize industries by increasing efficiency, reducing costs, and enhancing transparency.

At the heart of smart contracts was the Ethereum blockchain, which provided a decentralized platform for developers to create and deploy these digital agreements. The flexibility of Ethereum's scripting language allowed for a wide range of applications, from simple token transfers to complex decentralized applications (dApps). This innovation opened up new possibilities for automating processes and transactions in various sectors, including finance, supply chain management, and real estate.

Smart contracts offered several advantages over traditional agreements. First, they were tamper-proof and immutable, ensuring that once deployed, the terms could not be altered. This provided a higher level of security and trust compared to conventional contracts, which could be subject to manipulation or disputes. Second, smart contracts were transparent and publicly accessible, allowing all parties to verify the terms and conditions. This transparency reduced the likelihood of fraud and increased accountability.

Despite their potential, smart contracts faced several challenges. The complexity of writing and auditing smart contracts introduced the risk of bugs and vulnerabilities. High-profile incidents, such as the DAO hack in 2016, highlighted the importance of rigorous testing and security measures. Additionally, the legal status of smart contracts remained uncertain in many jurisdictions, raising questions about their enforceability and compliance with existing regulations.

As the technology continued to evolve, developers and legal experts worked together to address these challenges. New tools and frameworks emerged to simplify the creation and auditing of smart contracts, while regulatory bodies began to explore ways to integrate smart contracts into existing legal systems. The future of agreements was undoubtedly digital, and smart contracts were poised to play a central role in shaping this new landscape.

7

Chapter 7: DAOs: The New Organizational Model

Decentralized Autonomous Organizations (DAOs) represented a radical departure from traditional organizational structures. These digital entities, governed by smart contracts and decentralized decision-making processes, operated without centralized leadership or hierarchical management. DAOs leveraged blockchain technology to create transparent, efficient, and democratic organizations that could adapt to the rapidly changing digital landscape.

At the core of a DAO was a set of smart contracts that encoded the organization's rules and decision-making processes. Members of the DAO could propose and vote on changes, with the outcomes automatically enforced by the underlying code. This decentralized governance model ensured that all stakeholders had a voice and that decisions were made collectively, rather than by a select few.

The potential applications of DAOs were vast and varied. In the world of finance, DAOs could manage investment funds, allocate resources, and distribute profits transparently and efficiently. In the realm of social impact, DAOs could coordinate charitable initiatives, fund community projects, and support grassroots movements. The flexibility of the DAO model allowed it to be tailored to the specific needs and goals of any organization.

However, the rise of DAOs also raised important questions and challenges. The decentralized nature of these organizations made it difficult to hold individuals accountable for their actions, leading to potential governance issues and conflicts. Additionally, the legal status of DAOs remained uncertain in many jurisdictions, raising concerns about liability, regulatory compliance, and dispute resolution.

Despite these challenges, the promise of DAOs was undeniable. They represented a new way of organizing and collaborating, one that harnessed the power of blockchain technology to create more transparent, inclusive, and resilient entities. As DAOs continued to gain traction, they had the potential to redefine the very concept of an organization and pave the way for a new era of decentralized governance.

8

Chapter 8: Blockchain and Global Governance

Blockchain technology had far-reaching implications for global governance. By providing a transparent, secure, and tamper-proof system for recording transactions and data, blockchain offered the potential to enhance accountability, reduce corruption, and improve efficiency in public administration. The integration of blockchain into government processes and institutions could transform the way nations governed and interacted with their citizens.

One of the most promising applications of blockchain in governance was in the area of voting and elections. Traditional voting systems were often plagued by issues such as fraud, manipulation, and low voter turnout. Blockchain-based voting systems offered a solution by providing a transparent and verifiable record of votes, ensuring that the results were accurate and tamper-proof. This increased trust in the electoral process and encouraged greater citizen participation.

In addition to voting, blockchain technology could be used to improve the transparency and efficiency of public administration. By recording government transactions and processes on a blockchain, citizens could have greater visibility into how public funds were being allocated and spent. This increased transparency reduced the risk of corruption and mismanagement, fostering greater trust between governments and their citizens.

Blockchain also had the potential to streamline and enhance international cooperation. Cross-border transactions and agreements could be recorded on a shared blockchain, reducing the complexity and cost of international trade and diplomacy. This increased efficiency and transparency could foster greater collaboration and trust between nations, addressing global challenges such as climate change, poverty, and security.

However, the integration of blockchain into global governance was not without challenges. The technology was still relatively new, and its implementation required significant investment and expertise. Additionally, the decentralized nature of blockchain sometimes clashed with the centralized structures of traditional governments, leading to resistance and regulatory hurdles.

Despite these challenges, the potential benefits of blockchain in global governance were too significant to ignore. As nations and international organizations continued to explore and experiment with blockchain solutions, they had the opportunity to create more transparent, efficient, and accountable systems of governance that could better serve their citizens and address global challenges.

9

Chapter 9: The Impact on Traditional Industries

The rise of blockchain technology and cryptocurrencies had a profound impact on traditional industries, disrupting established business models and creating new opportunities for innovation. From finance and supply chain management to healthcare and real estate, blockchain's decentralized and transparent nature offered significant advantages that could transform the way industries operated.

In the financial sector, blockchain technology revolutionized the way transactions were conducted and recorded. Traditional banking systems, often burdened by inefficiencies and intermediaries, were challenged by the speed, security, and cost-effectiveness of blockchain-based solutions. Cryptocurrencies and decentralized finance (DeFi) platforms offered new ways for individuals and businesses to manage assets, access credit, and conduct cross-border transactions. This disruption forced traditional financial institutions to adapt, innovate, and explore partnerships with blockchain startups.

The supply chain industry also saw significant benefits from blockchain technology. By providing an immutable and transparent record of goods' provenance and movement, blockchain improved traceability and accountability. This increased visibility helped to reduce fraud, counterfeiting, and inefficiencies, ensuring that products were delivered safely and ethically. Companies like IBM and Walmart began implementing blockchain solutions to enhance their supply chain operations, demonstrating the technology's potential to drive industry-wide transformation.

In healthcare, blockchain technology offered the potential to improve patient data management and security. By creating a decentralized and tamper-proof record of medical histories, blockchain could ensure that patient data was accurate, accessible, and secure. This increased interoperability between healthcare providers, reducing errors and improving patient outcomes. Additionally, blockchain-enabled solutions could streamline clinical trials, improve drug traceability, and enhance the overall efficiency of the healthcare system.

The real estate industry also experienced disruption from blockchain technology. Smart contracts facilitated transparent and efficient property transactions, reducing the need for intermediaries and minimizing the risk of fraud. Blockchain-based platforms enabled fractional ownership of real estate, making property investment more accessible to a broader range of investors. This democratization of real estate investment had the potential to reshape the industry and create new opportunities for growth.

While the impact of blockchain on traditional industries was profound, it also posed challenges. The adoption of blockchain technology required significant investment in infrastructure, education, and regulatory compliance. Additionally, the transition from traditional systems to blockchain-based solutions was complex and required overcoming technical and cultural barriers.

Despite these challenges, the potential of blockchain to transform traditional industries was undeniable. As businesses continued to explore and implement blockchain solutions, they had the opportunity to create more efficient, transparent, and innovative operations that could drive long-term growth and success.

10

Chapter 10: The Financial Sector Transformed

The integration of blockchain technology into the financial sector marked a paradigm shift that transformed traditional banking and financial services. This transformation was driven by the fundamental principles of blockchain: decentralization, transparency, and security. As blockchain technology matured, it became clear that its impact would be far-reaching, revolutionizing the way financial institutions operated and interacted with their clients.

One of the most significant changes was the rise of decentralized finance (DeFi). DeFi platforms leveraged blockchain technology to create a wide range of financial services, including lending, borrowing, trading, and investing, without the need for traditional intermediaries like banks. These platforms offered greater accessibility, lower fees, and enhanced transparency compared to conventional financial services. As a result, DeFi gained rapid adoption and became a cornerstone of the new financial ecosystem.

Another key innovation was the development of stablecoins—cryptocurrencies pegged to the value of traditional assets like fiat currencies or commodities. Stablecoins addressed the issue of volatility that plagued many cryptocurrencies, providing a more stable and reliable medium of exchange. This innovation facilitated greater adoption of digital currencies in everyday transactions and cross-border payments, further integrating blockchain technology into the financial system.

Tokenization also emerged as a powerful tool for transforming financial assets. By representing real-world assets like stocks, bonds, and real estate as digital tokens on a blockchain, tokenization enabled fractional ownership and increased liquidity. This democratized access to investment opportunities and allowed a broader range of investors to participate in the financial markets. Tokenization also streamlined the issuance and trading of assets, reducing costs and increasing efficiency.

The financial sector's transformation was not without challenges. Regulatory bodies struggled to keep pace with the rapid development of blockchain technology, leading to uncertainty and fragmented approaches to regulation. Ensuring the security and scalability of blockchain networks was an ongoing concern, as high-profile hacks and scalability issues highlighted the need for robust solutions. Additionally, the integration of blockchain technology required significant investment in infrastructure and education.

Despite these challenges, the transformation of the financial sector was a testament to the disruptive power of blockchain technology. By embracing decentralization, transparency, and security, the financial industry was poised to create a more inclusive, efficient, and resilient ecosystem that could better serve the needs of a globalized world.

11

Chapter 11: From Wall Street to Silicon Valley

The convergence of finance and technology was epitomized by the rise of blockchain technology, bringing together the worlds of Wall Street and Silicon Valley. This fusion created a fertile ground for innovation, attracting a new breed of entrepreneurs, investors, and technologists who sought to redefine the future of finance and technology.

In the early days of blockchain, Wall Street's response was mixed. Traditional financial institutions were initially skeptical of cryptocurrencies and blockchain technology, viewing them as speculative and risky. However, as the technology matured and its potential became more evident, Wall Street began to take notice. Major financial institutions, including investment banks, hedge funds, and asset management firms, started exploring blockchain's applications and investing in blockchain startups.

The rise of blockchain technology also spurred the growth of the fintech sector. Silicon Valley, known for its culture of innovation and disruption, embraced blockchain as a catalyst for change. Tech giants like Google, Microsoft, and Facebook began investing in blockchain research and development, exploring its potential to transform various industries. Startups focused on blockchain technology emerged, attracting significant venture capital funding and driving further innovation.

The collaboration between Wall Street and Silicon Valley created a unique ecosystem where finance and technology intersected. This ecosystem fostered the development of new financial products and services, leveraging blockchain's capabilities to enhance efficiency, security, and transparency. Decentralized finance (DeFi) platforms, digital wallets, and blockchain-based payment systems became integral components of this new financial landscape.

However, the convergence of Wall Street and Silicon Valley also brought challenges. The regulatory environment remained complex and uncertain, with different jurisdictions taking varied approaches to blockchain regulation. The cultural differences between the traditional financial sector and the tech industry sometimes led to friction and misunderstandings. Additionally, the rapid pace of innovation created a need for continuous education and adaptation.

Despite these challenges, the collaboration between Wall Street and Silicon Valley represented a powerful force for change. By combining the financial expertise of Wall Street with the technological prowess of Silicon Valley, the blockchain revolution had the potential to create a more innovative, efficient, and inclusive financial system. As this convergence continued to evolve, it would shape the future of both industries and redefine the boundaries of possibility.

12

Chapter 12: Blockchain in Emerging Markets

The impact of blockchain technology was particularly profound in emerging markets, where traditional financial and institutional infrastructures were often underdeveloped or inefficient. Blockchain offered a unique opportunity to leapfrog legacy systems and create more inclusive, transparent, and efficient solutions for a wide range of challenges.

One of the most significant applications of blockchain in emerging markets was in the area of financial inclusion. A large portion of the population in these regions lacked access to traditional banking services, limiting their ability to save, borrow, and invest. Blockchain-based solutions, such as mobile wallets and decentralized finance (DeFi) platforms, provided accessible and affordable financial services to the unbanked and underbanked. This empowerment allowed individuals to participate in the global economy and improve their economic well-being.

Another key application of blockchain in emerging markets was in supply chain management. In regions where supply chains were often fragmented and opaque, blockchain technology offered a way to improve traceability, transparency, and efficiency. By recording every step of the supply chain on a blockchain, companies could ensure the authenticity and quality of products, reduce fraud, and increase accountability. This had significant implications for industries such as agriculture, pharmaceuticals, and manufacturing.

Blockchain also played a crucial role in addressing issues related to land ownership and property rights in emerging markets. In many regions, land records were poorly maintained, leading to disputes and insecurity of tenure. Blockchain-based land registries provided a secure and immutable record of property ownership, reducing the risk of disputes and enabling individuals to use their property as collateral for loans. This increased stability and economic opportunities for landowners.

The potential of blockchain in emerging markets extended to areas such as healthcare, education, and governance. Blockchain-based solutions could improve the management and security of patient records, enhance the transparency and efficiency of educational credentialing, and increase accountability in public administration. These applications had the potential to create significant social and economic benefits, improving the quality of life for millions of people.

However, the adoption of blockchain in emerging markets faced several challenges. The lack of infrastructure, digital literacy, and regulatory frameworks posed significant barriers to implementation. Additionally, the volatility of cryptocurrency markets and the complexity of blockchain technology created uncertainty and risk. Despite these challenges, the potential benefits of blockchain in emerging markets were too significant to ignore.

As governments, businesses, and international organizations continued to explore and invest in blockchain solutions, they had the opportunity to create more inclusive and sustainable development pathways. By leveraging blockchain's unique capabilities, emerging markets could overcome existing challenges and unlock new opportunities for growth and prosperity.

13

Chapter 13: Ethics and the Blockchain

The rise of blockchain technology brought with it a host of ethical considerations and dilemmas. As with any disruptive innovation, the implementation and adoption of blockchain had the potential to create both positive and negative impacts on society. Addressing these ethical concerns was crucial to ensuring that the technology was used responsibly and for the greater good.

One of the primary ethical considerations related to the use of blockchain was the issue of privacy. While blockchain offered increased transparency and accountability, it also raised concerns about the protection of personal data. Public blockchains, in particular, made transaction data publicly accessible, potentially compromising individuals' privacy. Balancing transparency with privacy was a delicate challenge that required careful consideration and the development of privacy-preserving technologies.

Another ethical concern was the environmental impact of blockchain, particularly related to the energy consumption of Proof of Work (PoW) consensus mechanisms. The energy-intensive nature of mining operations raised questions about the sustainability of blockchain technology. As the industry grew, it became imperative to explore and adopt more environmentally friendly consensus mechanisms, such as Proof of Stake (PoS), and to invest in renewable energy sources to mitigate the environmental footprint.

The issue of financial inclusion was also an important ethical consideration.

While blockchain had the potential to democratize access to financial services, there was a risk that the benefits of the technology would be concentrated among a small group of early adopters and tech-savvy individuals. Ensuring that blockchain solutions were accessible and inclusive was essential to fulfilling the technology's promise of empowerment and equality.

The rise of decentralized finance (DeFi) and cryptocurrencies also raised ethical questions about the potential for market manipulation, fraud, and the financing of illicit activities. The pseudonymous nature of blockchain transactions made it challenging to identify and prevent criminal activities. Developing robust regulatory frameworks and security measures was crucial to addressing these risks and ensuring the integrity of the blockchain ecosystem.

Additionally, the governance of blockchain networks and decentralized autonomous organizations (DAOs) presented ethical dilemmas related to accountability, transparency, and power dynamics. The decentralized nature of these entities made it difficult to hold individuals accountable for their actions, leading to potential governance issues and conflicts. Establishing clear governance frameworks and mechanisms for accountability was essential to addressing these challenges.

As blockchain technology continued to evolve and proliferate, it was crucial to engage in ongoing ethical reflection and dialogue. By addressing these ethical concerns proactively, the blockchain community could ensure that the technology was used responsibly and for the benefit of all. This required collaboration between developers, policymakers, and stakeholders to create a more ethical and sustainable blockchain ecosystem.

14

Chapter 14: Security and Privacy Concerns

As blockchain technology gained prominence, security and privacy concerns became paramount. While blockchain offered significant advantages in terms of transparency and immutability, it also introduced new risks and vulnerabilities that needed to be addressed to ensure the technology's safe and secure adoption.

One of the primary security concerns related to blockchain technology was the potential for hacking and cyberattacks. High-profile incidents, such as the Mt. Gox hack and the DAO hack, demonstrated the vulnerabilities of blockchain networks and smart contracts. These incidents highlighted the importance of robust security measures, including regular audits, code reviews, and the implementation of best practices for secure development. Ensuring the security of blockchain networks was a continuous process that required vigilance and adaptation to evolving threats.

Privacy was another critical concern in the blockchain ecosystem. Public blockchains, by design, made transaction data publicly accessible, raising questions about the protection of personal information. While transactions were pseudonymous, meaning they were not directly linked to real-world identities, sophisticated analysis techniques could potentially deanonymize users. To address these concerns, developers explored privacy-enhancing technologies, such as zero-knowledge proofs and confidential transactions, which allowed for private and secure transactions on public blockchains.

The issue of regulatory compliance also intersected with security and privacy concerns. Governments and regulatory bodies sought to balance the need for transparency and accountability with the protection of individual privacy and data security. This balancing act required the development of clear regulatory frameworks that addressed the unique characteristics of blockchain technology while ensuring compliance with existing laws and regulations. Collaboration between regulators, industry stakeholders, and the blockchain community was essential to create a secure and compliant ecosystem.

Security and privacy were not only technical challenges but also ethical considerations. Ensuring the responsible and ethical use of blockchain technology required a commitment to protecting users' rights and fostering trust within the ecosystem. This included developing standards and guidelines for data protection, implementing robust security measures, and promoting transparency and accountability in the development and deployment of blockchain solutions.

As blockchain technology continued to evolve and mature, addressing security and privacy concerns was critical to its long-term success and adoption. By prioritizing these issues, the blockchain community could create a more secure, private, and trustworthy ecosystem that could fully realize the technology's potential.

15

Chapter 15: The Road Ahead: Challenges and Opportunities

The future of blockchain technology was filled with both challenges and opportunities. As the technology continued to evolve and gain traction, it was essential to navigate the complexities and uncertainties that lay ahead while seizing the opportunities for innovation and growth.

One of the primary challenges facing the blockchain industry was scalability. As blockchain networks grew in size and usage, the limitations of current consensus mechanisms became apparent. High transaction fees, slow processing times, and network congestion were significant hurdles that needed to be addressed to ensure the technology's widespread adoption. Innovations such as sharding, layer-2 solutions, and new consensus mechanisms like Proof of Stake (PoS) offered promising avenues for scaling blockchain networks and improving their performance.

Regulatory uncertainty was another significant challenge. The rapid development of blockchain technology outpaced the ability of regulatory bodies to create comprehensive frameworks. This uncertainty created risks for businesses and investors, making it crucial to establish clear and consistent regulations that supported innovation while protecting consumers and maintaining financial stability. Collaboration between regulators, industry stakeholders, and the blockchain community was essential to create a balanced and forward-looking regulatory environment.

Interoperability was also a critical issue that needed to be addressed. The blockchain ecosystem was composed of numerous independent networks, each with its own protocols and standards. Ensuring seamless communication and interaction between these networks was essential for realizing the full potential of blockchain technology. Interoperability solutions, such as cross-chain protocols and interoperability standards, aimed to bridge the gaps between different blockchain networks and create a more cohesive and connected ecosystem.

Despite these challenges, the opportunities presented by blockchain technology were immense. From decentralized finance (DeFi) and digital identity to supply chain management and healthcare, blockchain had the potential to transform industries and create new economic models. The continued development and adoption of blockchain solutions could drive innovation, increase efficiency, and empower individuals and communities worldwide.

The road ahead required a collaborative and inclusive approach that brought together developers, businesses, regulators, and users. By working together to address the challenges and seize the opportunities, the blockchain community could build a more equitable, transparent, and resilient future. As the technology continued to evolve, the possibilities were limited only by the imagination and ingenuity of those who embraced the promise of blockchain.

16

Chapter 16: Case Studies: Successes and Failures

The journey of blockchain technology was marked by both successes and failures, each offering valuable lessons and insights into the potential and pitfalls of this disruptive innovation. Examining case studies of notable blockchain projects provided a deeper understanding of the factors that contributed to their success or failure and the broader implications for the industry.

One of the most successful blockchain projects was Bitcoin, the first cryptocurrency and the catalyst for the blockchain revolution. Bitcoin's success was attributed to its robust and secure protocol, strong community support, and the visionary leadership of its pseudonymous creator, Satoshi Nakamoto. Despite its early challenges and skepticism, Bitcoin gained widespread adoption and became a store of value and medium of exchange. Its success demonstrated the potential of decentralized digital currencies and paved the way for the broader blockchain ecosystem.

Ethereum was another notable success story. Launched in 2015 by Vitalik Buterin, Ethereum introduced the concept of smart contracts and provided a decentralized platform for developing decentralized applications (dApps). Ethereum's flexibility and innovation attracted a vibrant developer community and led to the creation of numerous successful projects, including decentralized finance (DeFi) platforms and non-fungible tokens (NFTs). Ethereum's success showcased the versatility and potential of blockchain technology beyond digital currencies.

However, not all blockchain projects were successful. The DAO (Decentralized Autonomous Organization) was one of the most high-profile failures in the blockchain space. Launched in 2016 on the Ethereum blockchain, the DAO aimed to create a decentralized investment fund governed by its members. Despite raising significant funds, the DAO fell victim to a critical vulnerability in its smart contract code, resulting in a hack that drained millions of dollars' worth of Ether. The incident led to a contentious hard fork of the Ethereum blockchain and highlighted the importance of rigorous security audits and testing in blockchain development.

Another notable failure was the Mt. Gox exchange, once the largest Bitcoin exchange in the world. Mt. Gox experienced a series of security breaches and operational issues, culminating in its bankruptcy in 2014 after losing approximately 850,000 bitcoins. The collapse of Mt. Gox underscored the need for robust security measures, transparent operations, and regulatory oversight in the cryptocurrency industry.

These case studies offered valuable lessons for the blockchain community. Success in the blockchain space required a combination of strong technical foundations, community support, security measures, and regulatory compliance. Failures, while unfortunate, provided opportunities for learning and improvement, driving the evolution and maturation of the industry.

By examining the successes and failures of blockchain projects, the community could better navigate the challenges and opportunities ahead. Each experience, whether positive or negative, contributed to the collective knowledge and resilience of the blockchain ecosystem, paving the way for a brighter and more innovative future.

17

Chapter 17: Conclusion: Embracing the New Rules of Global Leadership

As blockchain technology continued to reshape the world, it was clear that the new rules of global leadership were being written. The rise of the sovereign algorithm, the emergence of blockchain billionaires, and the decentralized revolution had fundamentally altered the dynamics of power, wealth, and governance. Embracing these new rules required a willingness to adapt, innovate, and collaborate in a rapidly changing digital landscape.

The transformative potential of blockchain technology lay in its ability to democratize access to information, resources, and opportunities. By eliminating intermediaries, increasing transparency, and enhancing security, blockchain had the power to create a more equitable and inclusive world. The decentralized ethos of blockchain challenged traditional power structures and empowered individuals and communities to take control of their destinies.

However, the journey was not without its challenges. The road ahead required addressing issues related to scalability, security, privacy, and regulatory compliance. Navigating these complexities demanded a collaborative approach that brought together diverse stakeholders, including developers, businesses, regulators, and users. By working together, the blockchain community could create a robust and resilient ecosystem that harnessed the technology's potential for positive change.

The new rules of global leadership also required ethical considerations and a commitment to responsible innovation. Ensuring the protection of privacy, promoting financial inclusion, and addressing environmental impacts were essential to the long-term success and sustainability of blockchain technology. By prioritizing these ethical concerns, the blockchain community could build trust and credibility, fostering a positive and lasting impact on society.

As the world embraced the new rules of global leadership, the possibilities were endless. The blockchain revolution was still in its early stages, and its full potential had yet to be realized. By continuing to explore, experiment, and innovate, the blockchain community could create a future where technology served the greater good and empowered individuals and communities worldwide.

In conclusion, the rise of the sovereign algorithm and the new rules of global leadership represented a profound shift in the way the world operated. Embracing these changes required a bold vision, a collaborative spirit, and a commitment to ethical principles. As the blockchain revolution continued to unfold, it held the promise of creating a more transparent, inclusive, and equitable world, redefining the boundaries of possibility and shaping the future of global society.

The Sovereign Algorithm: Billionaires, Blockchain, and the New Rules of Global Leadership

In "The Sovereign Algorithm: Billionaires, Blockchain, and the New Rules of Global Leadership," embark on a captivating journey through the transformative world of blockchain technology and its profound impact on global power dynamics. This groundbreaking book delves into the rise of the sovereign algorithm—an unyielding digital force reshaping the foundations of wealth, governance, and society.

Through a series of meticulously crafted chapters, the book explores the birth of cryptocurrency and the rise of blockchain billionaires, who harness the power of decentralized technology to redefine traditional industries and create new economic paradigms. It examines the decentralized revolution, where power is transferred from centralized institutions to individuals, fostering greater transparency, efficiency, and inclusion.

From the dawn of blockchain and the potential of smart contracts to the ethical considerations and security challenges that accompany this disruptive innovation, "The Sovereign Algorithm" provides a comprehensive and insightful analysis of the blockchain ecosystem. The book also highlights real-world case studies of successes and failures, offering valuable lessons for navigating the complexities of this rapidly evolving landscape.

As the world embraces the new rules of global leadership, this book serves as a guide to understanding the profound implications of blockchain technology and its potential to create a more equitable, transparent, and resilient future. Whether you are a technologist, entrepreneur, policymaker, or curious reader, "The Sovereign Algorithm" offers a thought-provoking and enlightening exploration of the blockchain revolution and its impact on our world.

www.ingramcontent.com/pod-product-compliance
Lightning Source LLC
LaVergne TN
LVHW020459080526
838202LV00057B/6054